HINCHINGBROOKE SCHOOL
LIBRARY RESOURCE CENTRE

WITHDRAWN FROM STOCK

Religious Stories

The Life of Muhammad

Maryam Davies

Illustrated by
Khalida Rahman
and
Chris Rothero

Religious Stories

Buddhist Stories
Chinese Stories
Creation Stories
Guru Nanak and the Sikh Gurus
Hindu Stories
The Life of the Buddha
The Life of Jesus
The Life of Muhammad
The Lives of the Saints
Old Testament Stories

Edited by: Stephen Setford
First published in 1987 by
Wayland (Publishers) Ltd
61 Western Road, Hove,
East Sussex BN3 1JD, England

© Copyright 1987 Wayland (Publishers) Ltd

British Library Cataloguing in
 Publication Data
Davies, Maryam
 The life of Muhammad. – (Religious stories series)
 1. Muhammad (*Prophet*) – Biography – Juvenile literature 2. Muslims – Saudi Arabia – Biography – Juvenile literature
 I. Title II. Rahman, Khalida
 III. Rothero, Chris IV. Series
 297'.63 BP75
 ISBN 0-85078-904-4

Phototypeset by
Kalligraphics Ltd, Redhill, Surrey
Printed in Italy by
G. Canale & C.S.p.A., Turin
Bound in the U.K. by
The Bath Press, Avon

Publishers' note
Many of the illustrations in this book are based around, or contain, Arabic calligraphy. The meanings of these calligraphies are shown in small type at the foot of the text columns. The cover calligraphy reads: 'Muhammad is the Prophet of God'.

Contents

The birth of Muhammad   8

Muhammad's early life   16

The first revelation   24

The escape from Makkah   32

The Muslims reach Madinah   40

The return to the Ka'bah   48

Glossary   60

Notes for teachers   61

Books to read   62

The birth of Muhammad

Aminah and her husband 'Abd Allah were very happy. They were expecting their first baby. They lived in the Arabian city of Makkah, but 'Abd Allah had gone to Syria with a caravan of camels.

Makkah was a busy trading centre with many caravans of camels passing through. Aminah would often watch the merchants unloading spices and silks from China and India, which the camels had brought from ships at the port of Aden. Once the camels were reloaded again they set off on their long journeys to Palestine and Syria.

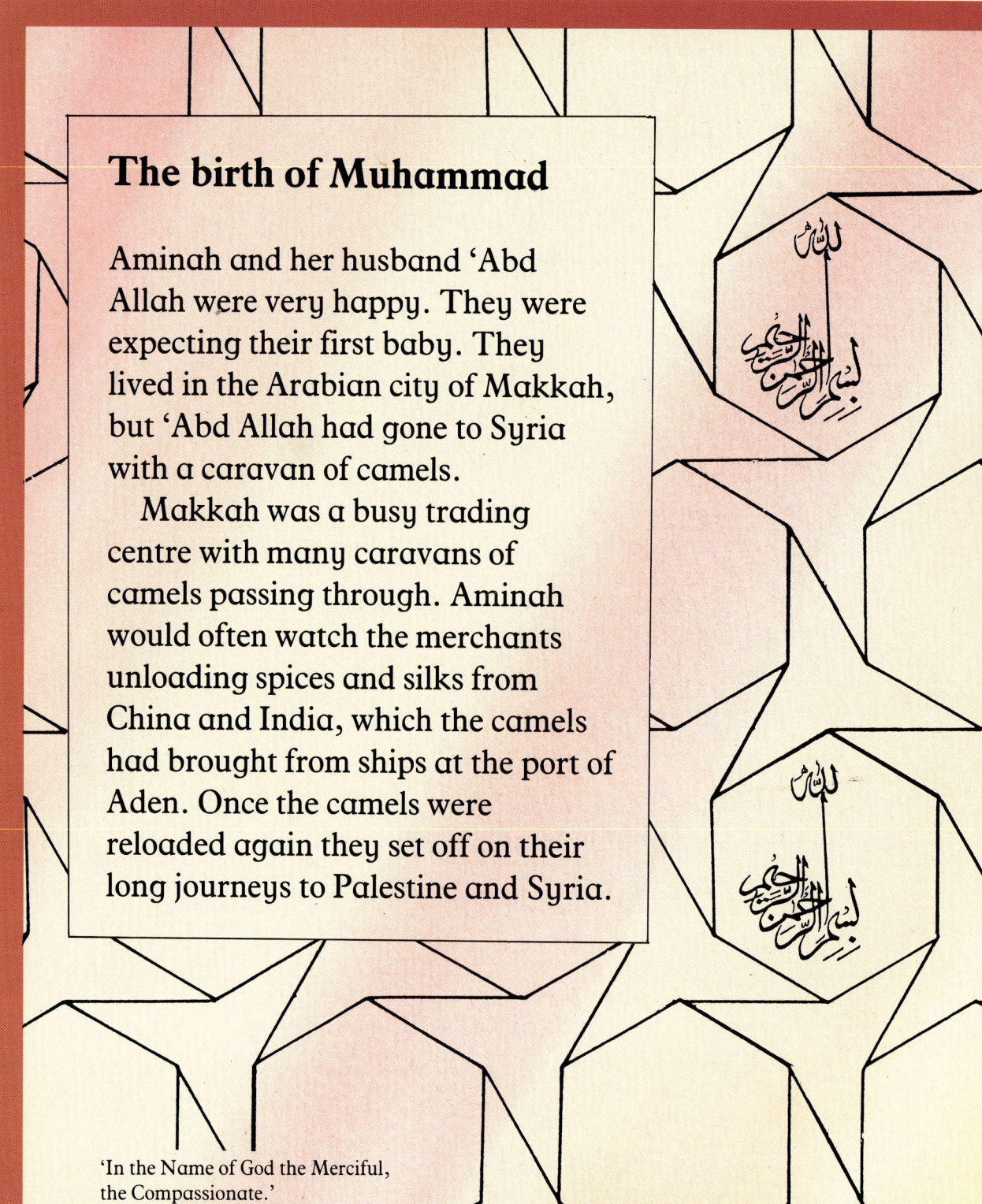

'In the Name of God the Merciful, the Compassionate.'

Arab tribes from the surrounding desert came to Makkah to trade. They also came to visit a shrine called the Ka'bah. At the shrine they prayed to gods and goddesses. They asked them for help with all their problems.

Although the shrine had been built originally for the worship of the one true God, it was now filled with statues and idols of these false gods. Only a few people remembered that long ago prophets such as Adam, Moses, Abraham and Jesus had taught that there was really only one God.

When 'Abd Allah's caravan of camels arrived back in Makkah, he was nowhere to be seen. The merchants told his father, 'Abd al-Muttalib, that 'Abd Allah had been taken ill so he had stayed behind in the town of Yathrib.

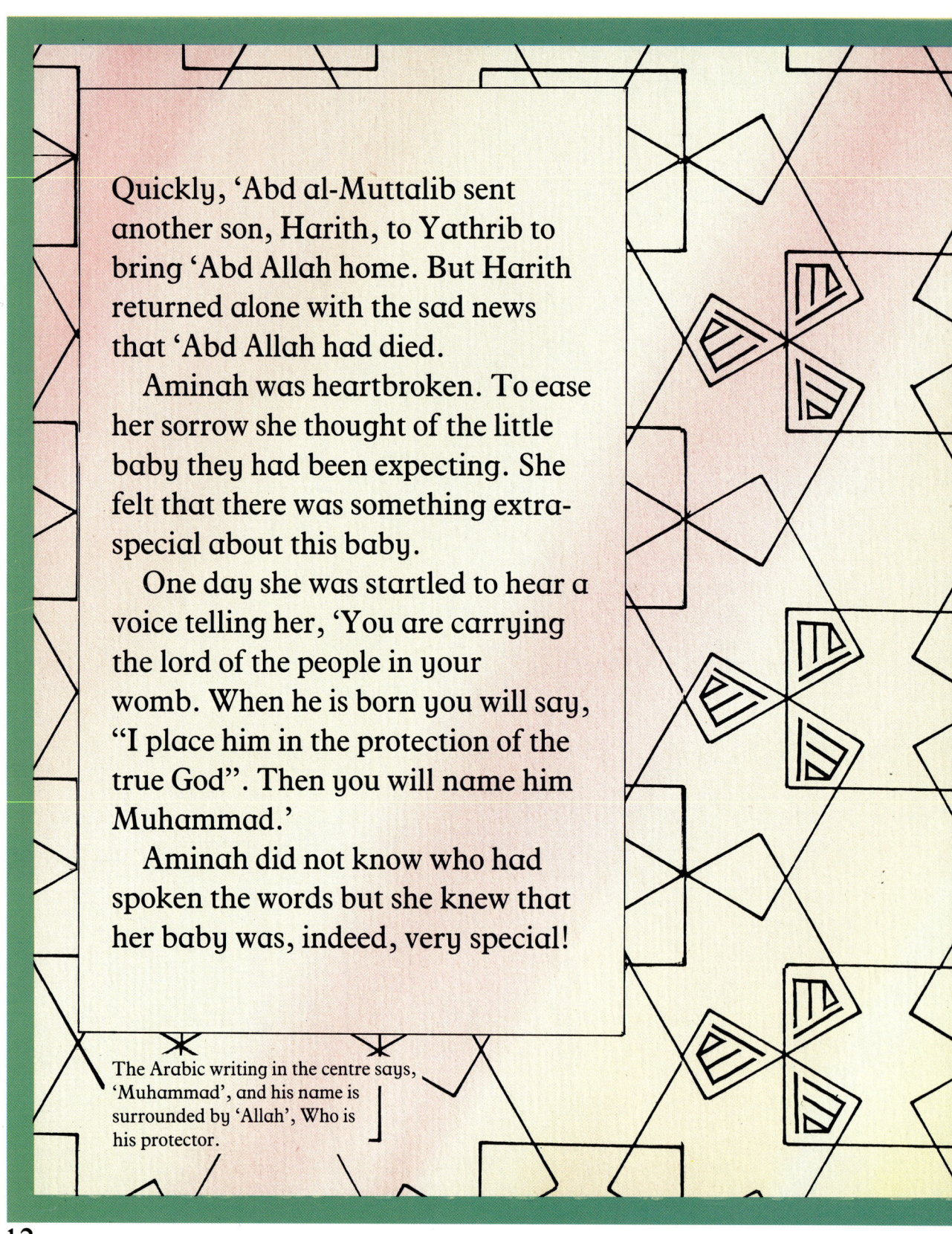

Quickly, 'Abd al-Muttalib sent another son, Harith, to Yathrib to bring 'Abd Allah home. But Harith returned alone with the sad news that 'Abd Allah had died.

Aminah was heartbroken. To ease her sorrow she thought of the little baby they had been expecting. She felt that there was something extra-special about this baby.

One day she was startled to hear a voice telling her, 'You are carrying the lord of the people in your womb. When he is born you will say, "I place him in the protection of the true God". Then you will name him Muhammad.'

Aminah did not know who had spoken the words but she knew that her baby was, indeed, very special!

The Arabic writing in the centre says, 'Muhammad', and his name is surrounded by 'Allah', Who is his protector.

'Abd al-Muttalib was the grandfather of Aminah's baby. Aminah sent for him as soon as her baby was born. He took his little grandson in his arms and carried him straight to the Ka'bah.

'Abd al-Muttalib was one of the few Makkans who believed in the true God. Now he praised Allah, which is the Arabic word for God, for sending the precious child he was holding. And the baby was named Muhammad just as the voice had told Aminah.

'Praise belongs to God'
(repeated three times).

اَلْحَمْدُ لِلهِ

اَلْحَمْدُ لِلهِ

اَلْحَمْدُ لِلهِ

Muhammad's early life

Muhammad's father had died before he was born and his mother died when he was still a little boy. Her death left him in the care of his grandfather, 'Abd al-Muttalib, who had always been fond of his little grandson.

'Abd al-Muttalib was an old man, however, and when Muhammad was still only eight years old, he died. Just before his death, 'Abd al-Muttalib asked his son, Abu Talib, who was Muhammad's uncle, to look after the young boy. Abu Talib and his wife, Fatimah, brought up Muhammad with their own sons.

As he grew up, Muhammad enjoyed helping his uncle. He herded the sheep and goats on the hills around Makkah. When he was older he went further afield on long journeys with Abu Talib.

'Muhammad' (peace and the Mercy of God be upon him).

When his uncle took him to Syria with a caravan of camels he met a monk named Bahirah. The monk recognised Muhammad as one of God's chosen prophets. He advised Abu Talib to take good care of his young nephew. 'There is a great future in store for him,' said Bahirah, 'so hurry back to your country with him.'

By the time Muhammad was twenty years old he was already well known for his honesty and perfect behaviour.

He was so trustworthy that his uncle, Abu Talib, was able to recommend him to a wealthy widow named Khadijah, who wanted a responsible man to take charge of her camel caravans.

Khadijah was so impressed with Muhammad when he bought and sold goods for her in Syria, that she made him a proposal of marriage after he returned to Makkah. She told him, 'I love you for your trustworthiness and for the beauty of your character and the truth in your speech.'

Muhammad and Khadijah were married for twenty-five years. They had six children, two boys and four girls, but both their baby sons died.

Muhammad remembered how kind his uncle Abu Talib had been to him when he was an orphan. When he noticed that Abu Talib's family had grown larger than he could afford to support, Muhammad suggested that the youngest son, 'Ali, should move in with himself and Khadijah. From then on, 'Ali became part of Muhammad's own family.

'Muhammad' (peace and the Mercy of God be upon him).

Sometimes Muhammad would leave his wife at home in Makkah and go off by himself into the hills. He liked to be alone to think about the city life he saw in Makkah. He wondered why so many people visited the Ka'bah. Did they really believe that statues carved by human hands could answer their prayers?

Muhammad was certain that only Allah should be worshipped and that the idols in the Ka'bah and in people's houses were useless.

He also believed that Allah would not accept the bad behaviour of the city people. They were greedy and corrupt. Their great riches also encouraged them to drink and gamble. They were even making money by selling small copies of the large idols, for people to worship in their homes.

'Where will it all end?' Muhammad asked himself.

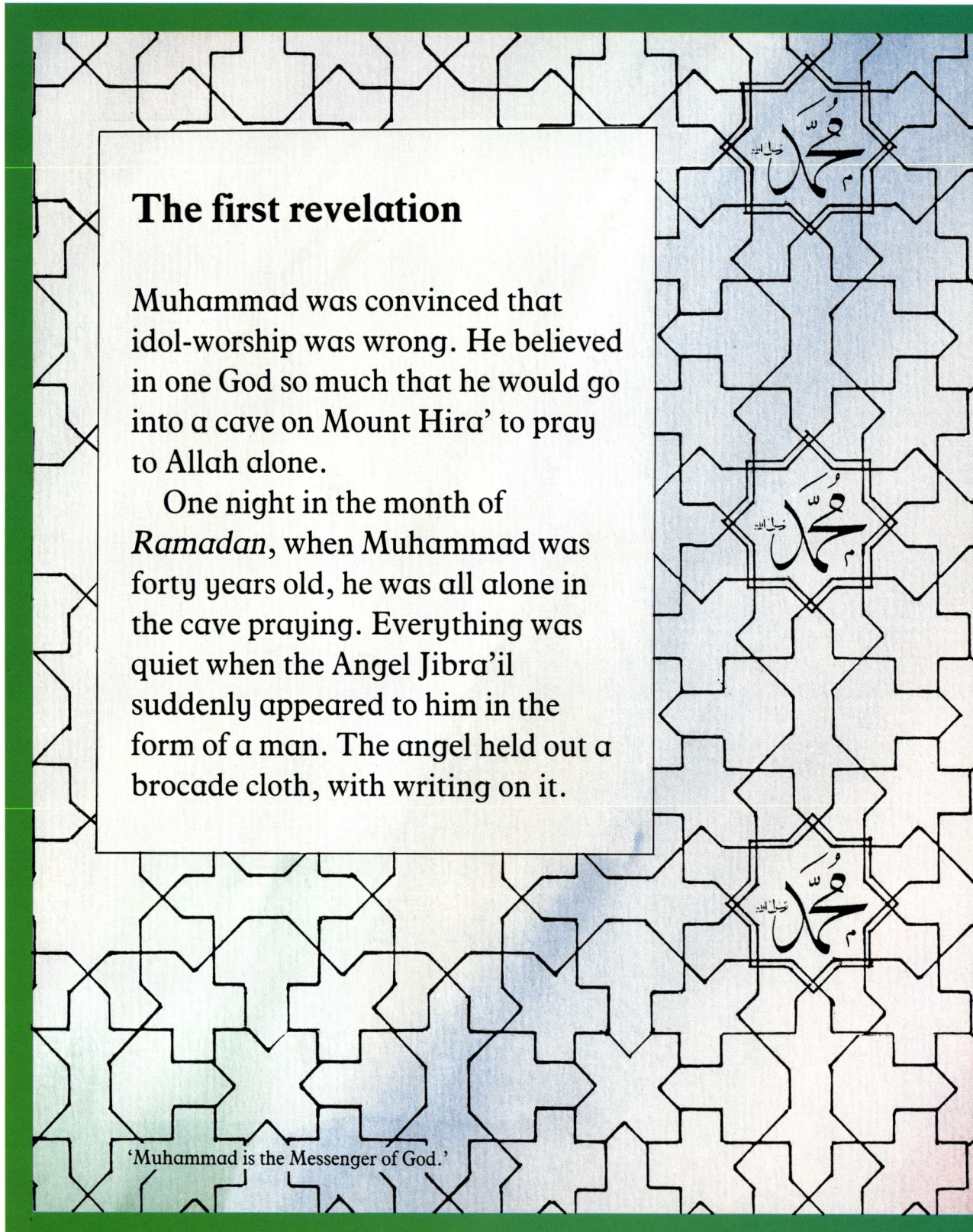

The first revelation

Muhammad was convinced that idol-worship was wrong. He believed in one God so much that he would go into a cave on Mount Hira' to pray to Allah alone.

One night in the month of *Ramadan*, when Muhammad was forty years old, he was all alone in the cave praying. Everything was quiet when the Angel Jibra'il suddenly appeared to him in the form of a man. The angel held out a brocade cloth, with writing on it.

'Muhammad is the Messenger of God.'

The angel told Muhammad to read from the cloth. 'I cannot read,' replied Muhammad.

Again the angel told Muhammad to read, and again he insisted that he could not. Each time Muhammad said that he could not read the angel squeezed him.

For a third time the angel commanded Muhammad to read, saying, 'Read, in the name of your Lord Who created! Created man from a clot of blood. Read, and your Lord is the Most Bounteous, Who taught by the use of the pen, taught man that which he knew not.'

Suddenly Muhammad found he could read after all! Describing the experience later, he said, 'It was as though the words were written on my heart.'

'Read! in the Name of your Lord who created! Created man from a clot of blood. Read, and your Lord is the Most Bounteous, Who taught by the use of the pen, taught man that which he knew not.'
(The Holy *Qur'an*, 96. 1–4)

He was very badly shaken by what had happened. He started to rush down the mountainside towards home but half way down he heard a voice above him saying: 'O Muhammad. You are the messenger of God and I am Jibra'il.' Whichever way Muhammad turned, all that he could see was Jibra'il.

When he at last arrived home, he told the whole story to Khadijah. She had watched her husband searching for truth for many years. Now she realized that Allah had chosen this man, whom she knew and loved, to be His prophet.

The revelations continued for twenty-three more years until the Prophet's death. Every one of Allah's words was recorded in writing. Muhammad remembered how, in the cave, the Angel Jibra'il had told him that Allah taught people what they did not know 'by the use of the pen'.

'Muhammad is the Messenger of God.'

All the revelations were written down and collected together. They still remain unchanged in a book called the *Qur'an*, which is the Arabic word for 'a reading'.

In the *Qur'an* Allah answered all the questions troubling the Prophet Muhammad. In His revelations Allah confirmed that He alone created the world. He also created people and all the animals and plants.

Allah commanded that He alone should be worshipped and obeyed. He declared that idols were just as useless as the Prophet had always suspected. In the *Qur'an* Allah also revealed that people who always do their best to obey Him will be rewarded when they die. However, those who ignore Him and behave badly will be punished. It was Allah who chose the name Islam for this new teaching.

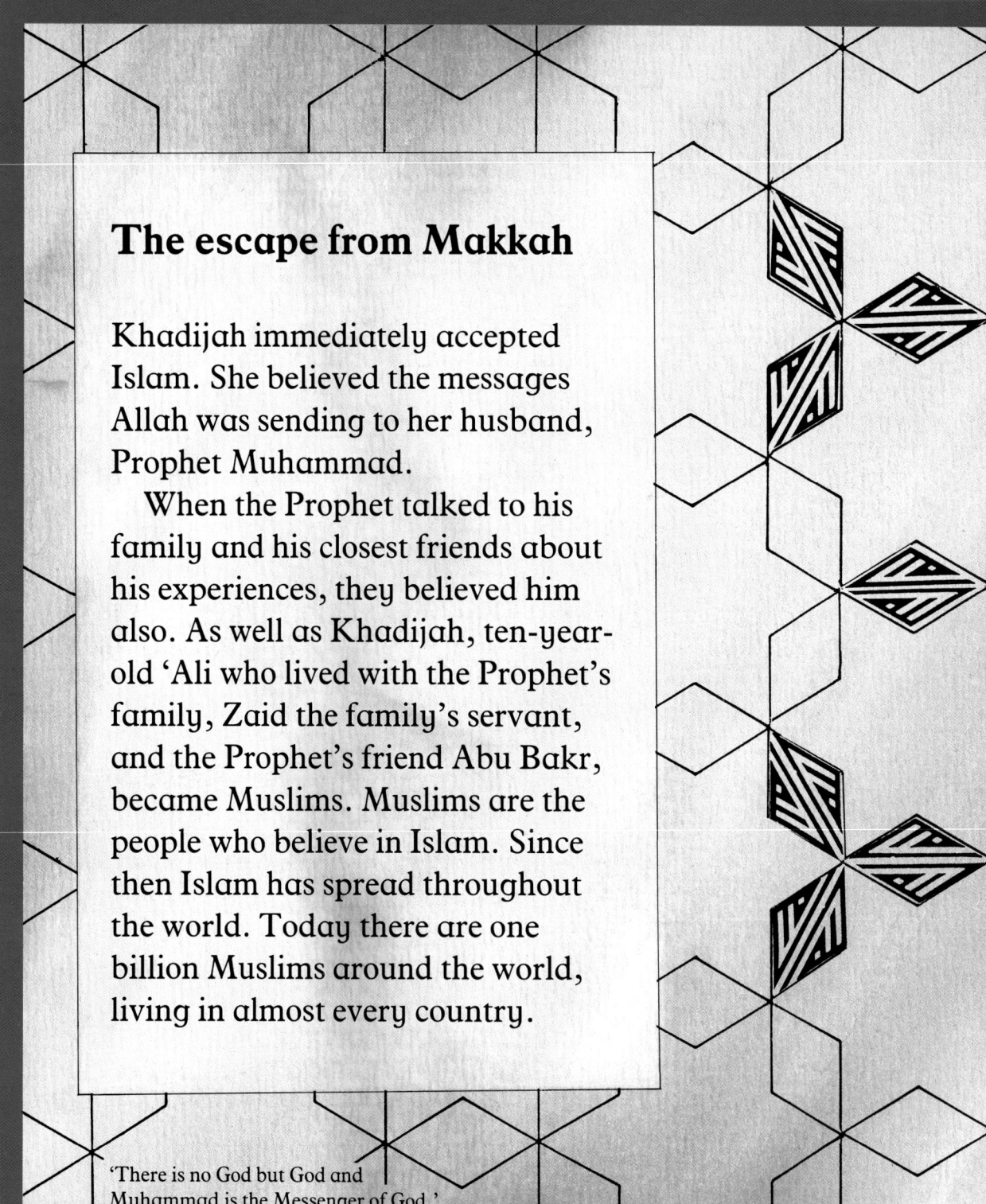

The escape from Makkah

Khadijah immediately accepted Islam. She believed the messages Allah was sending to her husband, Prophet Muhammad.

When the Prophet talked to his family and his closest friends about his experiences, they believed him also. As well as Khadijah, ten-year-old 'Ali who lived with the Prophet's family, Zaid the family's servant, and the Prophet's friend Abu Bakr, became Muslims. Muslims are the people who believe in Islam. Since then Islam has spread throughout the world. Today there are one billion Muslims around the world, living in almost every country.

'There is no God but God and Muhammad is the Messenger of God.'

But, in those early days, the rich Makkans did not want to hear about Allah's revelations. Instead, they wanted to keep their own power over the people. If people started believing in a god who said that worshipping idols was wrong, they would soon lose their power and wealth.

The powerful Quraysh, the Prophet's own tribe, turned against him. The tribe's leaders decided to destroy the new Islamic faith. Eventually, no one in Makkah who believed in the true God was safe.

Because of this the Prophet encouraged the Makkan Muslims to move to Yathrib. Quraysh leaders were angry when they discovered what was happening. They feared that if the Muslims went to Yathrib to settle, the new community would grow stronger and stronger, and become an even worse threat to the Makkans.

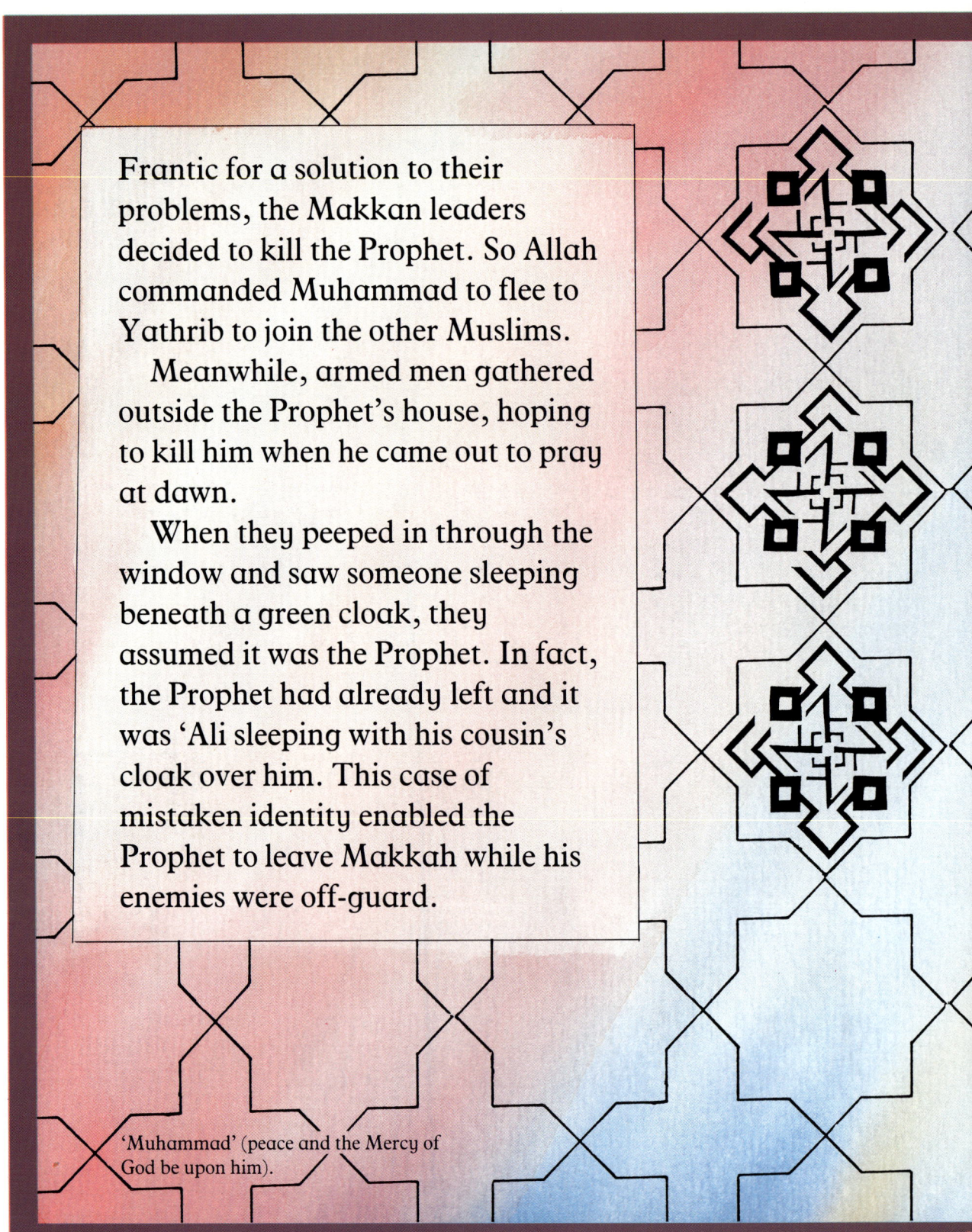

Frantic for a solution to their problems, the Makkan leaders decided to kill the Prophet. So Allah commanded Muhammad to flee to Yathrib to join the other Muslims.

Meanwhile, armed men gathered outside the Prophet's house, hoping to kill him when he came out to pray at dawn.

When they peeped in through the window and saw someone sleeping beneath a green cloak, they assumed it was the Prophet. In fact, the Prophet had already left and it was 'Ali sleeping with his cousin's cloak over him. This case of mistaken identity enabled the Prophet to leave Makkah while his enemies were off-guard.

'Muhammad' (peace and the Mercy of God be upon him).

He hurried to the home of his friend, Abu Bakr, who had two camels waiting. The Prophet climbed on to one camel and Abu Bakr and his son 'Abd Allah got on to the other. Together they rode south, towards a place in the mountains where they could hide. Two white rock doves followed them along the sandy track out of Makkah.

The armed men waiting outside the Prophet's home were very angry when they found that it was 'Ali and not the Prophet sleeping under the green cloak. They offered a reward of one hundred camels to anyone who could capture the Prophet. Naturally this handsome reward attracted hundreds of men, on foot and on horseback, determined to find the Prophet so that they could claim the camels.

They were confused by the many tracks which criss-crossed the desert, so they sent for a tracker to help them to find which path the Prophet had taken.

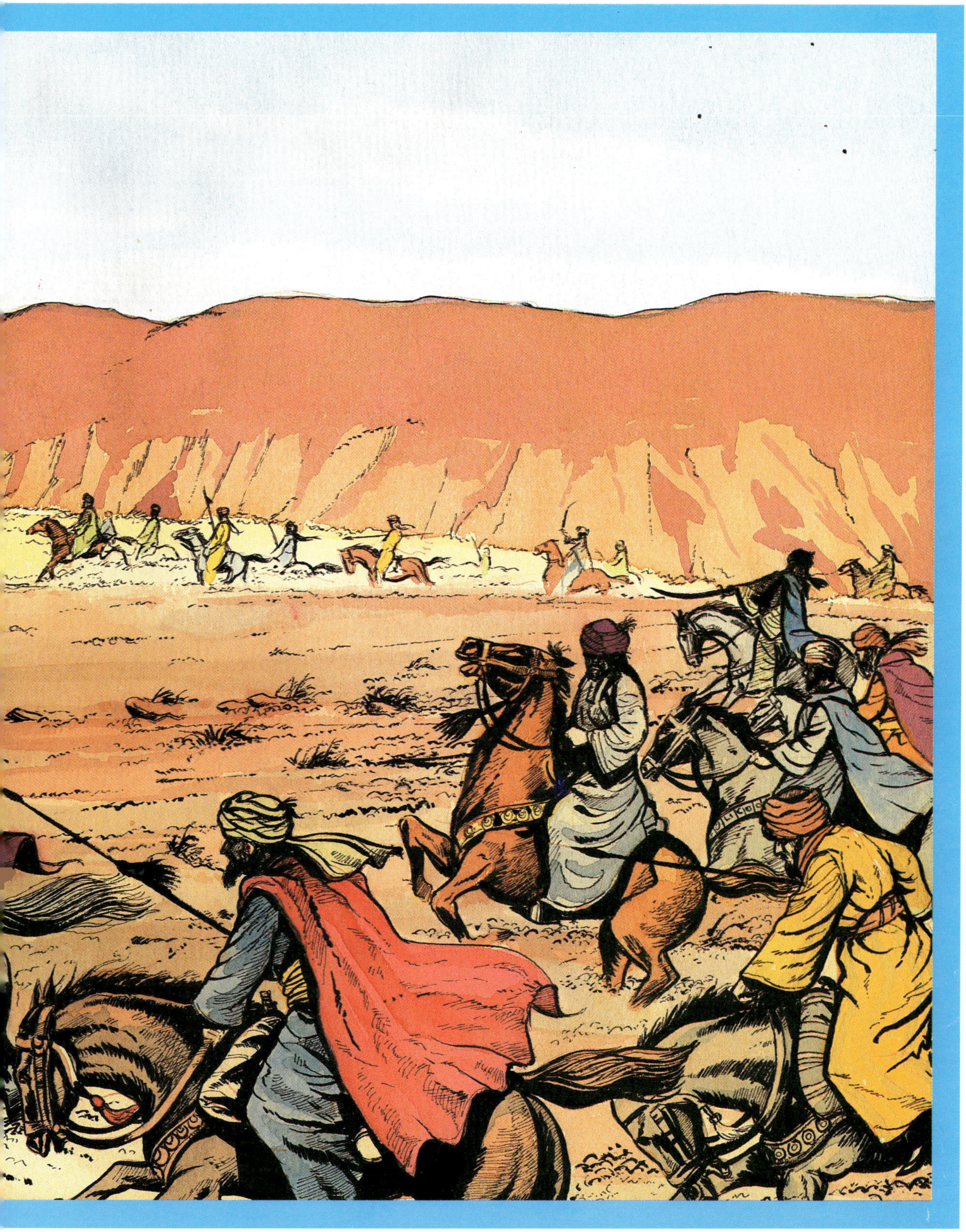

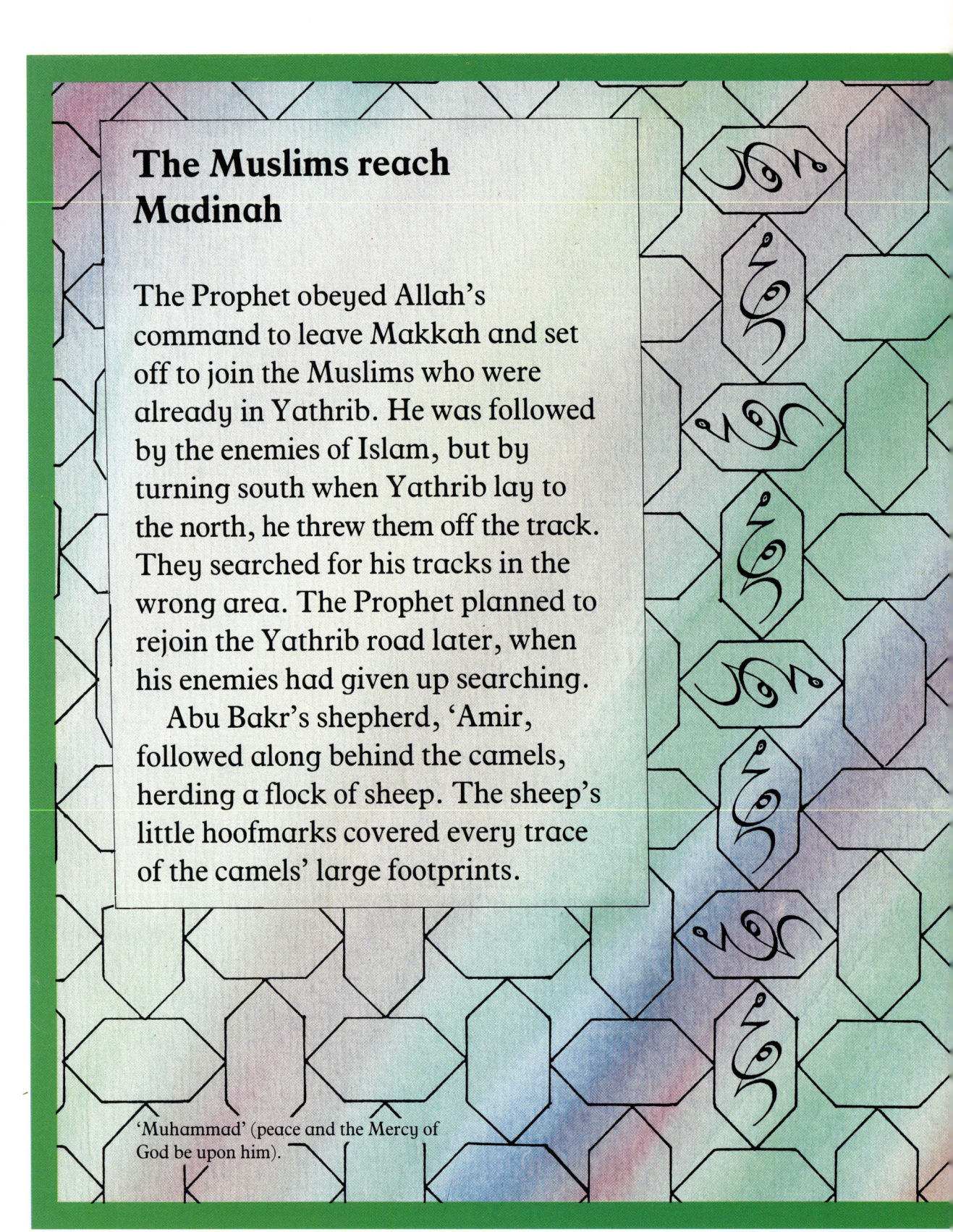

The Muslims reach Madinah

The Prophet obeyed Allah's command to leave Makkah and set off to join the Muslims who were already in Yathrib. He was followed by the enemies of Islam, but by turning south when Yathrib lay to the north, he threw them off the track. They searched for his tracks in the wrong area. The Prophet planned to rejoin the Yathrib road later, when his enemies had given up searching.

Abu Bakr's shepherd, 'Amir, followed along behind the camels, herding a flock of sheep. The sheep's little hoofmarks covered every trace of the camels' large footprints.

'Muhammad' (peace and the Mercy of God be upon him).

41

42

After travelling for five miles the Prophet and his friends found safety in a cave on Mount Thawr. The two rock doves which had followed them rested nearby.

Abu Bakr sent 'Abd Allah back down to Makkah with the camels. Each night 'Abd Allah returned to the cave, along with his sister Asma', with food for the Prophet and their father. 'Amir also continued to go to the cave daily with milk from the sheep. The sheep stirred up all the visitors' footprints when he drove them past the cave.

In the cave a little spider played its part in helping the Prophet. It started to spin a web right across the cave's entrance which was already partly hidden by some bushes.

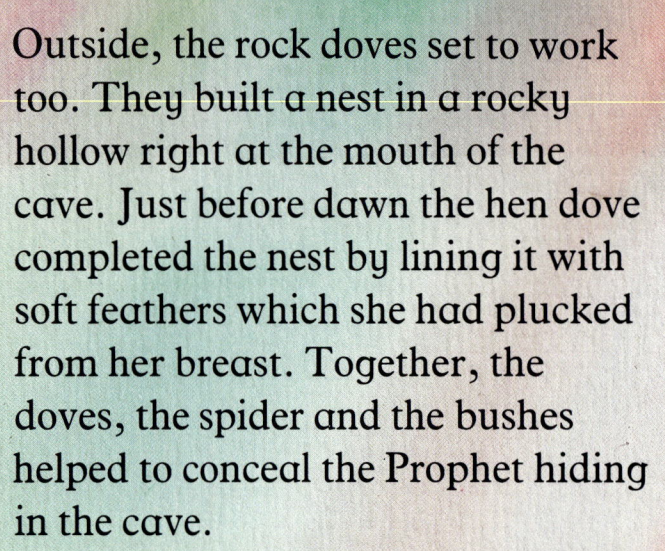

Outside, the rock doves set to work too. They built a nest in a rocky hollow right at the mouth of the cave. Just before dawn the hen dove completed the nest by lining it with soft feathers which she had plucked from her breast. Together, the doves, the spider and the bushes helped to conceal the Prophet hiding in the cave.

The Makkans searched for many days, getting closer and closer to the Prophet's hiding place. Before long they came right up to the cave entrance, their weapons at the ready in case the Prophet was inside.

Raising his sword, the leader shouted back to the others, 'Muhammad and his friends are surely hidden inside the cave.'

Just as he spoke the hen dove flew up from her nest right into his face. He looked down at the nest. 'No one can have got into this cave without treading on it,' he thought.

'Muhammad' (peace and the Mercy of God be upon him).

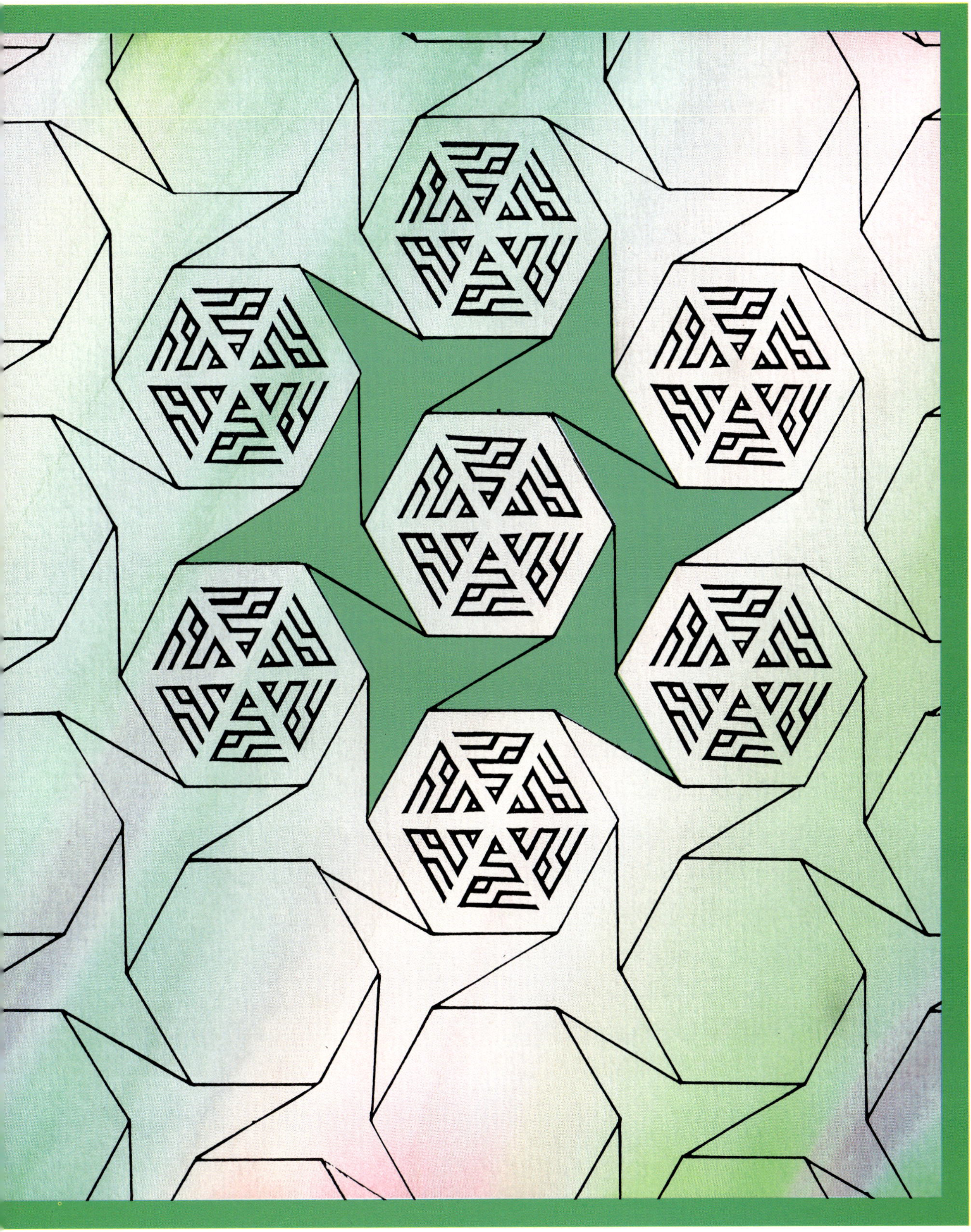

The enemies stared at the entrance to the cave. They saw the spider dangling on a silken thread from the web. They also saw the nest. They turned on the tracker angrily.

'Fancy leading us to this cave!' they shouted. 'It's obvious that no one has been into it for years!' They trudged back down the mountain, disappointed and frustrated that they had been led along the wrong path.

That night the Prophet and Abu Bakr left the cave. They went down to meet 'Abd Allah, Asma' and 'Amir who were on their way up the mountain on their nightly visit. In the valley the camels were waiting to continue the journey to Yathrib.

Yathrib was later renamed al-Madinah, which is Arabic for 'the city'. The Prophet's journey to Madinah from Makkah is called the *Hijrah*.

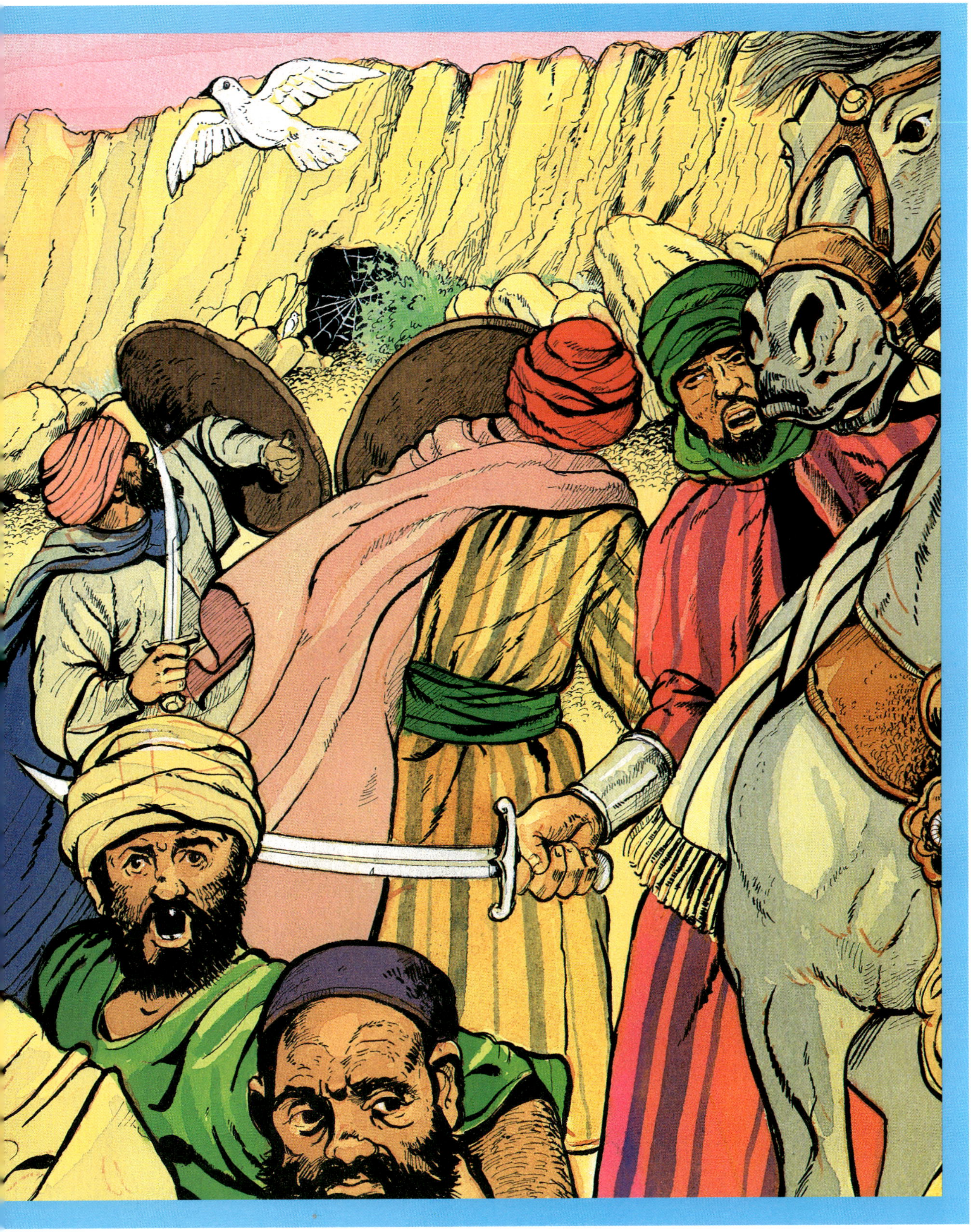

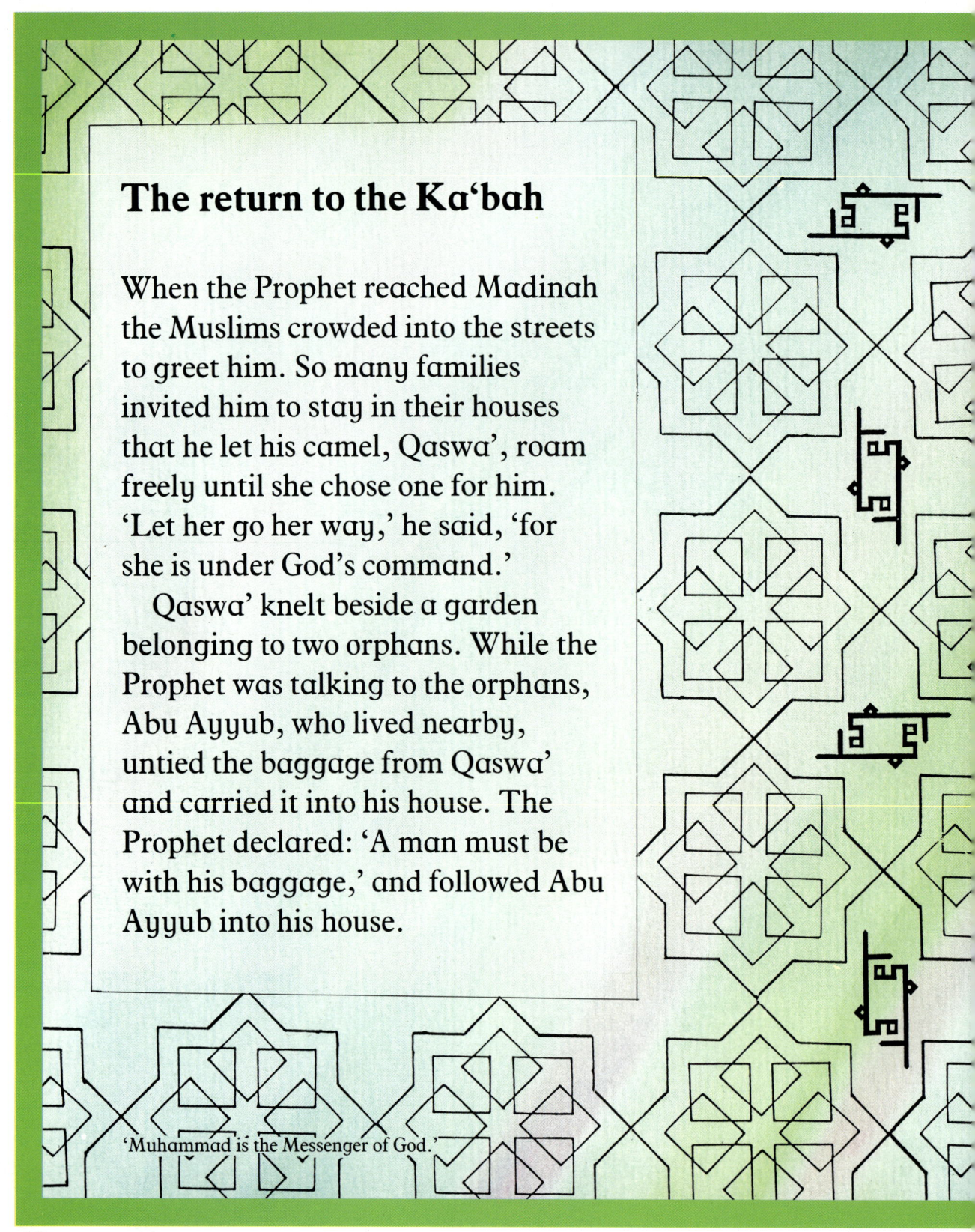

The return to the Ka'bah

When the Prophet reached Madinah the Muslims crowded into the streets to greet him. So many families invited him to stay in their houses that he let his camel, Qaswa', roam freely until she chose one for him. 'Let her go her way,' he said, 'for she is under God's command.'

Qaswa' knelt beside a garden belonging to two orphans. While the Prophet was talking to the orphans, Abu Ayyub, who lived nearby, untied the baggage from Qaswa' and carried it into his house. The Prophet declared: 'A man must be with his baggage,' and followed Abu Ayyub into his house.

'Muhammad is the Messenger of God.'

محمّد رسول الله

A mosque was built in the garden where Qaswa' had first rested. It was large enough to hold all the Muslims in Madinah when they gathered together, five times each day, for worship.

The Muslims received all their teachings from Allah in revelation after revelation. They were told what was good for them and what was forbidden. They were told to pray regularly, give to the poor and fast during *Ramadan*, whilst hoarding money, drinking alcohol and gambling were forbidden.

Allah also warned them of Islam's enemies. Islam was still a threat to the greedy, corrupt people whose power was based on idol-worship. These people were determined to destroy the Muslims and their faith.

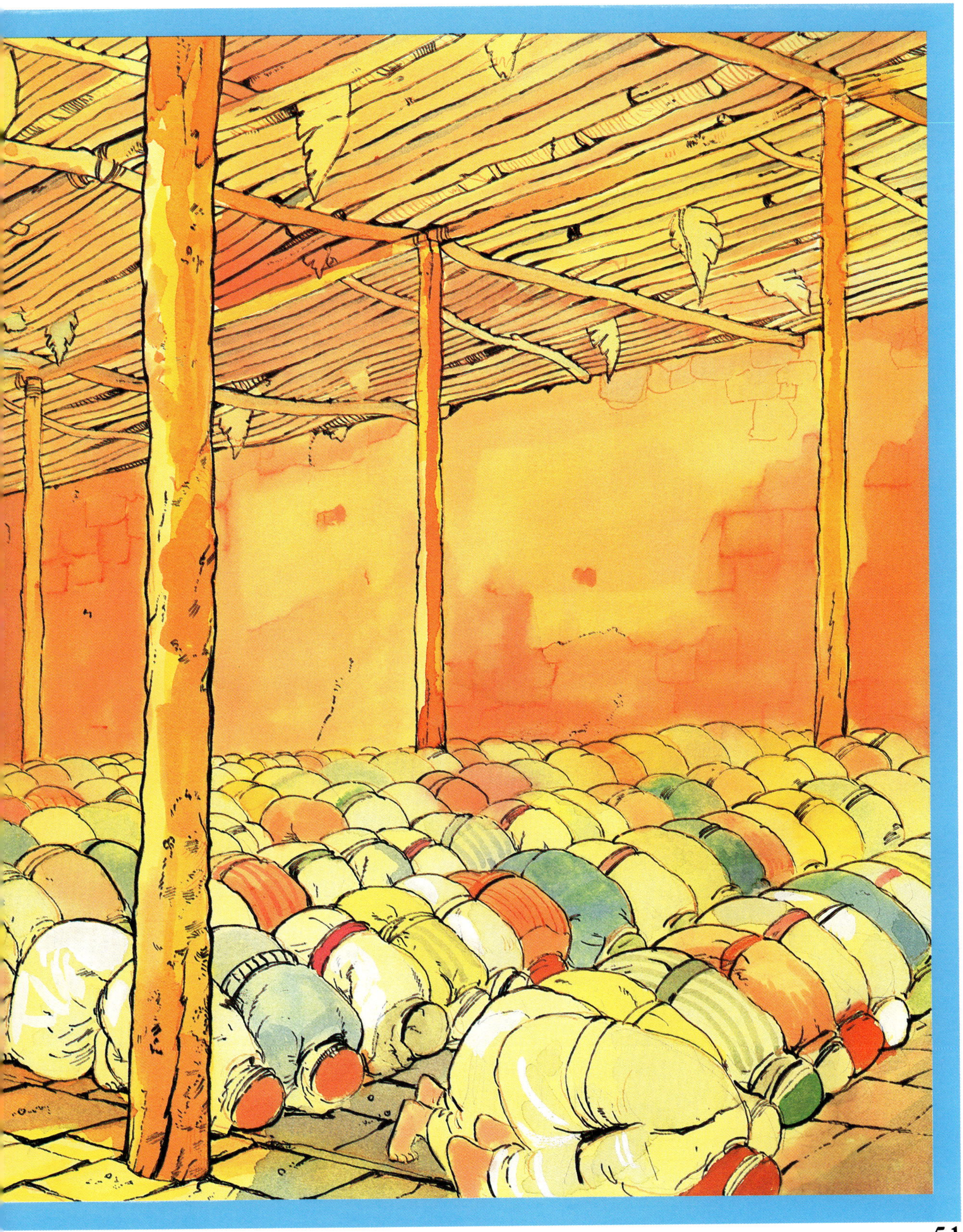

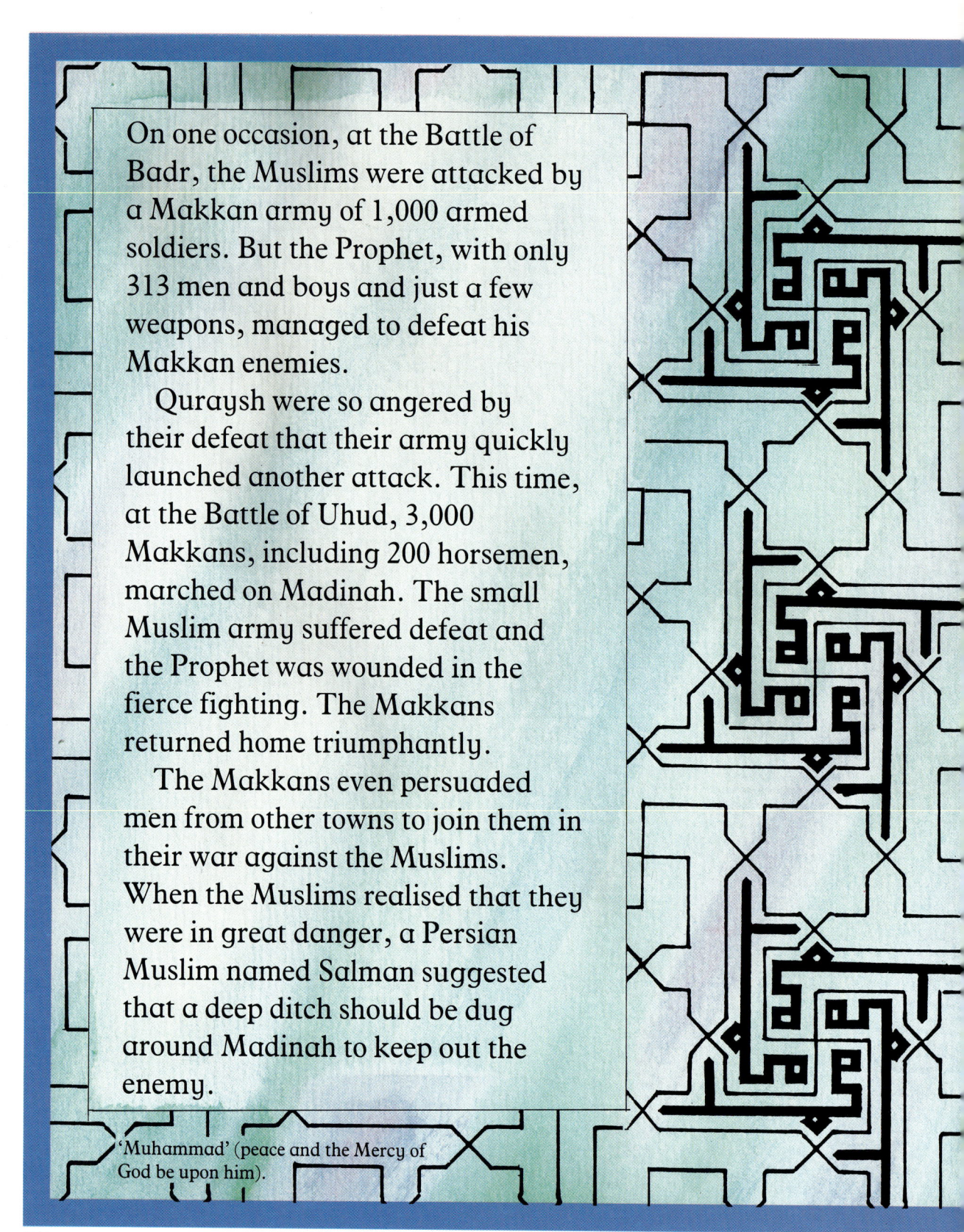

On one occasion, at the Battle of Badr, the Muslims were attacked by a Makkan army of 1,000 armed soldiers. But the Prophet, with only 313 men and boys and just a few weapons, managed to defeat his Makkan enemies.

Quraysh were so angered by their defeat that their army quickly launched another attack. This time, at the Battle of Uhud, 3,000 Makkans, including 200 horsemen, marched on Madinah. The small Muslim army suffered defeat and the Prophet was wounded in the fierce fighting. The Makkans returned home triumphantly.

The Makkans even persuaded men from other towns to join them in their war against the Muslims. When the Muslims realised that they were in great danger, a Persian Muslim named Salman suggested that a deep ditch should be dug around Madinah to keep out the enemy.

'Muhammad' (peace and the Mercy of God be upon him).

53

54

Salman's idea worked. The Makkans were stopped by the ditch and could not carry out their planned attack. For a month the Makkan army waited outside the ditch for an opportunity to enter Madinah. The soldiers ran low on food. They became so desperate that finally they decided to attack at night, despite the deep ditch.

The Muslims were very anxious, especially when the weather began to get worse. Cold, wet days were followed by strong winds which rose so high that they reached the force of a hurricane. The rain fell in torrents. It was only when the storm had eased that the Muslims discovered it was the Makkans who had suffered most in the storm. All the Makkan tents had been blown away and the soldiers were running off in terror and confusion.

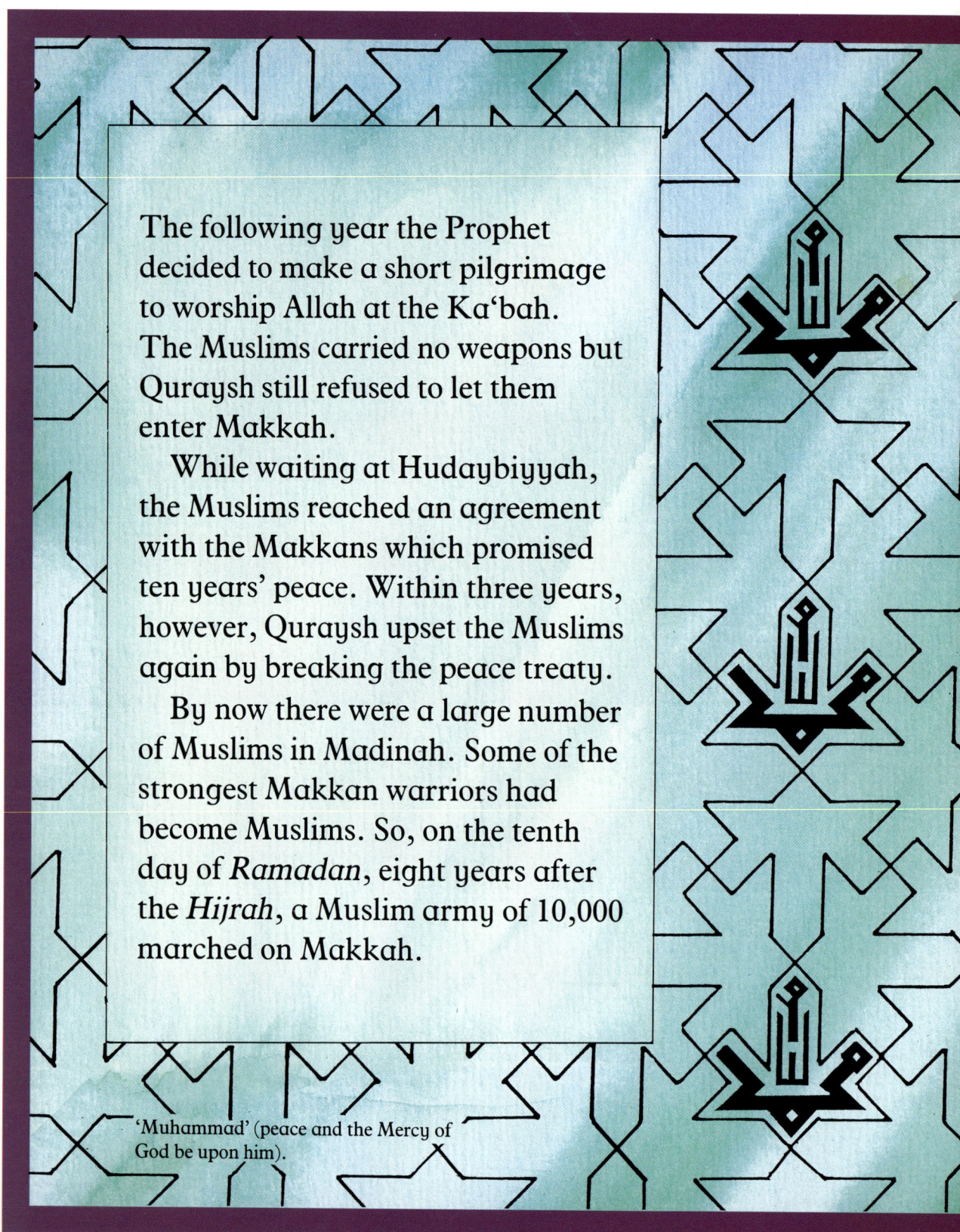

The following year the Prophet decided to make a short pilgrimage to worship Allah at the Ka'bah. The Muslims carried no weapons but Quraysh still refused to let them enter Makkah.

While waiting at Hudaybiyyah, the Muslims reached an agreement with the Makkans which promised ten years' peace. Within three years, however, Quraysh upset the Muslims again by breaking the peace treaty.

By now there were a large number of Muslims in Madinah. Some of the strongest Makkan warriors had become Muslims. So, on the tenth day of *Ramadan*, eight years after the *Hijrah*, a Muslim army of 10,000 marched on Makkah.

'Muhammad' (peace and the Mercy of God be upon him).

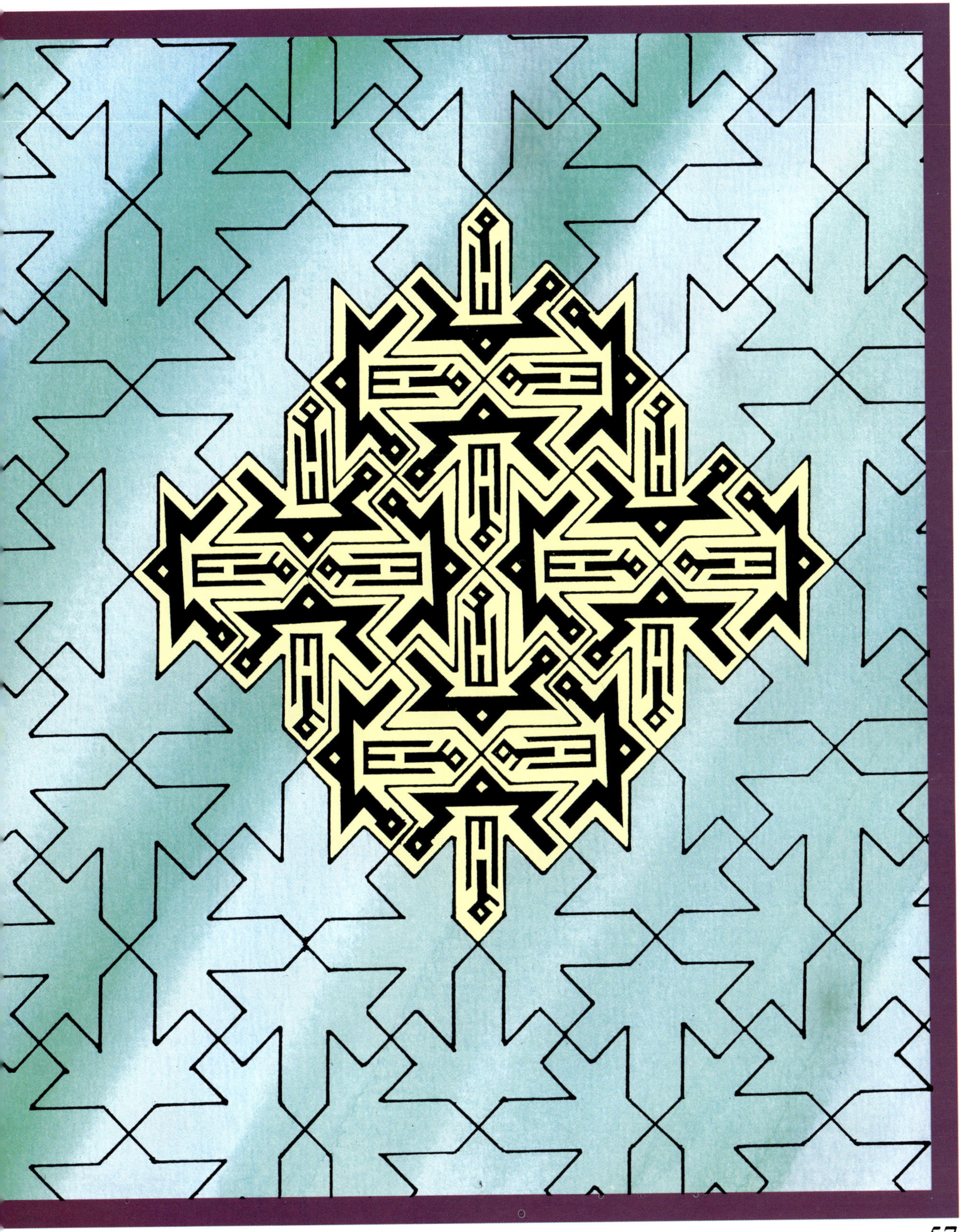

As the Muslims approached the city, the Makkans rushed inside their homes to safety. But the Prophet only wanted peace. Riding on Qaswa', he went to the Ka'bah straight away. There, he shouted: *'Allahu Akbar.'* Soon the whole city was echoing these words, which mean 'God is greatest'.

The Prophet ordered that all the idols in Makkah be destroyed. From that moment, people would only worship the one true God.

For three more years the Prophet led the Muslim community as it grew larger and larger.

When he died his mission was complete. He had spent twenty-three years as one of God's messengers, receiving direct guidance from Allah. In the *Qur'an*, Allah says that His messenger Muhammad is 'a blessing for the universe'.

'God is Greater.'

اللهُ أكبرُ

Glossary

Allah   The Arabic word for God which is always used by Muslims.
Angel   A messenger from God, or one of a class of spiritual beings who wait upon God.
Bounteous   Generous, giving freely.
Brocade   Cloth which is woven with a raised pattern.
Caravan   A long line of traders or other travellers journeying together through the desert, often with camels.
False gods or idols   Objects mistakenly worshipped, often sculpted to look like human or animal figures.
Hijrah   The year 622CE when the Prophet Muhammad arrived in Madinah from Makkah to establish the first Muslim community. The Muslim calendar starts from this date.
Islam   The Arabic word meaning submission to the Will of God.
Jibra'il   The angel who brought the revelation from God to the Prophet Muhammad. 'Jibra'il' is the Arabic spelling of the biblical name 'Gabriel'.
Ka'bah   A cubic construction covered with a black cloth, built by the Prophet Abraham in Makkah. It is the focus of the Muslims' annual pilgrimage; it is also the point to which all Muslims turn when praying.
Madinah   The city, formerly called Yathrib, in which the first Muslims established an Islamic State.
Makkah   The birthplace of the Prophet Muhammad in Saudi Arabia and the holiest place for Muslims.
Merchant   A person who buys and sells goods for profit.
Muslims   Followers of Islam; those who try to live according to God's guidance in the *Qur'an*. They believe in God and that the Prophet Muhammad was God's messenger. They also believe that Islam is their path to peace.
Prophet   A person through whom God expresses His will.
Qur'an   The sacred book for Muslims, each word of which was revealed by God. It was sent down to the Prophet Muhammad through the Angel Jibra'il. The Arabic text has remained unaltered for 1,400 years.
Quraysh   The noble tribe into which the Prophet Muhammad was born in 571CE.
Ramadan   The ninth month of the Muslim calendar. During *Ramadan* Muslims fast from dawn to sunset every day. The *Qur'an* was revealed to Prophet Muhammad during this month.
Revelation   God's disclosure of His own nature and purpose for mankind.
Shrine   A place of worship associated with a sacred person or object.
Worship   To show deep religious devotion to God.

Notes for teachers

The total Muslim population of the world is approximately one billion (a thousand million), which is roughly the same as the Christian population. Islam is a faith which is not confined to geographical territory, race, colour or language. Instead, Muslims are found in practically every country. All Muslims believe in the same five pillars of Islam: the belief in Allah and that Muhammad is His prophet; regular worship; the payment of alms; the *Hajj* (the pilgrimage to Makkah) and fasting during the month of *Ramadan*.

The stories in this book have been taken from the *Qur'an*, Martin Lings' *Muhammad, His Life Based on the Earliest Sources* (see further reading list) and traditional Muslim tales. It is customary, after using the name of the Prophet Muhammad, to write or say the honorific phrase, 'Peace be upon him'. Due to limited space, these words have been omitted from the text, although they can be inserted when reading the stories aloud in class or at home. When considering how to use these stories in the classroom, teachers may find it useful to enlist the help of a willing Muslim parent. In this way, a sympathetic approach, appreciated by Muslim parents, can quite easily be achieved.

Islamic art

The most important belief in Islam is that there is one God, which is the basic idea of monotheism. To further this belief, representational art – particularly with regard to the Prophet, his family and his companions – is disapproved of and in some Muslim sects forbidden, because a person could err by coming to worship that form. Instead, Islamic art turned to geometry to express the underlying order in the creation of the universe. As this order can be seen in the structure of geometry and because all geometric forms are generated from a single point, it is considered to be the best method of symbolizing the Creator who is One, and from Whom all things generate.

Muslim festivals

Muslim festivals are observed according to the Islamic calendar, which is based on lunar months. As the lunar year is shorter than the solar year by about ten days, it is impossible to give any dates on the Gregorian calendar which are permanent fixtures. The date of *Ramadan* ('The Month of the Heat') thus varies annually, and can occur in winter or summer.

In 1986, the Prophet Muhammad's birthday (*Milad-an-Nabi*) was celebrated on 15 November and *Ramadan* began on 9 May. At the end of the month-long fast during *Ramadan*, the feast day called *Eid al Fitr* is celebrated. It is a day of thanksgiving and happiness; prayer at the mosque, exchanging gifts and greetings, and visiting friends and relations are all part of the celebrations.

Books to read

For teachers and older readers
Ahmad, Khurshid, *Islam: its Meaning and Message* (1976)
Ali, Abdullah Yusuf, *The Glorious Qur'an* (The Islamic Foundation, 1978)
Darsh, S. M., *Muslims in Europe* (1980)
Haykal, Muhammad Husayn, *The Life of Muhammad*
　(American Trust Publications)
Lings, Martin, *Muhammad, His Life Based on the Earliest Sources*
　(Allen & Unwin, 1983)
McDermott, M. Y. and Ahsan, M. M., *The Muslim Guide*
　(The Islamic Foundation, 1980)
Nasr, S. H., *Ideals and Realities of Islam* (Unwin Paperbacks, 1979)
Sarwar, Ghulam, *Islam, Beliefs and Teachings* (Muslim Education Trust, 1982)
The Study of Al-Qur'an, Lessons 1–16 (Al-Qur'an Society, 1980–86)

For younger readers
Ahsan, M. M., *Muslim Festivals* (Wayland, 1985)
Al Hoad, Abdul Latif, *Islam* (Wayland, 1986)
Blakeley, Madeline, *Nahda's Family* (A & C Black, 1977)
Dennifer, Ahmad von, *Islam for Children* (The Islamic Foundation, 1981)
Guellowz, Eddedine, *Mecca: the Muslim Pilgrimage* (Paddington Press, 1977)
Kayoni, Mohammed Saleem, *Love all Creatures* (The Islamic Foundation, 1981)
Kayani, Mohammed Saleem, *The Meaning of the Glorious Qur'an in Current
　English* (Al-Kitab Publications, 78 Gillespie Road, London N5 1LN)
McDermott, Mustafa Yusuf, *Muslim Nursery Rhymes*
　(The Islamic Foundation, 1981)
Tames, Richard, *The Muslim World* (MacDonald, 1982)
Tarantino, Mardijah A., *Marvellous Stories from the Life of Muhammad*
　(The Islamic Foundation, 1982)

Useful addresses
Islamic Book Centre
120 Drummond Street, London NW1 2HL

The Islamic Foundation
223 London Road, Leicester LE2 1ZE

Muslim Information Services
223 Seven Sisters Road, London N4